French - Urdu

LEARNING FLASHCARDS

FOR BABIES TODDLERS

alligator

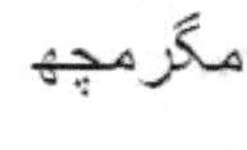

مگرمچھ

The alligator is having a party.

fourmi

چیونٹی

The ant is red.

ours

ریچھ

The bear loves you.

abeille

مکھی

The bee is saying hello.

oiseau

پرندہ

The bird is flying.

papillon

تتلی

The butterfly is pretty.

chameau

اونٹ

The camel has a hump.

chat

کیٹ

The cat is happy.

dinosaure

ڈائناسور

The dinosaur is laying eggs.

poulet

چکن

The chicken is dancing.

vache

گائے

The cow has a bell.

cerf

برن

The reindeer has a toy.

chien

كتا

The dog has two floppy ears.

dauphin

ڈالفن

The dolphin is swimming.

canard

بطخ

The duck has a bow.

aigle

عقاب

The eagle is looking for food.

l'éléphant

باتھی

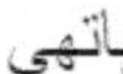

The elephant is sitting.

poisson

مچھلی

The fish is a clownfish.

libellule

ڈریگن فلائی

The dragonfly is blue.

renard

لومڑی

The fox has a red nose.

grenouille

مینڈک

The frog is smiling.

girafe

جراف

The giraffe has a long neck.

chèvre

بکرا

The goat has a beard

ver de terre

کیڑا

The worm is in the apple

poule

مرغی

The hen has chicks.

hippopotame

ہپپو پوٹیموس

The hippo is big.

cheval

گھوڑا

The horse is fast.

kangourou

کنگارو

The kangaroo has a baby.

chaton

بلی کے بچے

The kitten is playing.

lion

شیر

The lion has a mane.

homard

لابسٹر

The lobster is red.

singe

بندر

The monkey has a tail.

poulpe

آکٹپس

The octopus has food.

hibou

اللو

The owls have big eyes.

panda

پانڈا

The panda wears a diaper.

porc

سور

The pig is fat and pink.

chiot

كتے

The dog is brown.

lapin

خرگوش

The rabbit has a carrot.

rat

چوہا

The mouse is writing something.

crabe

کیکڑے

The crab has two pinchers.

requin

شارک

The shark is scary.

mouton

بھیڑ

The sheep are very fluffy.

escargot

سست

The snail is slow.

serpent

سانپ

The snake has poison.

araignée

مکڑی

The spider is purple.

écureuil

گلہری

The squirrel has a nut.

tigre

چیتا

The tiger has a red bow.

tortue

کچھی

The turtle has a shell.

loup

بھیڑیا

The wolf is smiling.

zèbre

زیبرا

The zebra is black and white.

dinde

ترکی

The turkey has two legs.

coq

مرغ

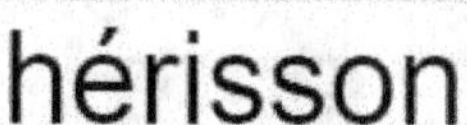

The rooster will crow.

perroquet

طوطا

The parrot is colorful.

hérisson

ہیج ہاگ

The hedgehog has apples.

pomme

سیب

The apple has a leaf.

abricot

خوبانی

The apricot is yellow.

avocat

ایوا کاڈو

The avocado has a nut.

banane

کیلا

The banana is yellow.

la mûre

بلیک بیری

There are a lot of blackberries.

cassis

کالی کشمش

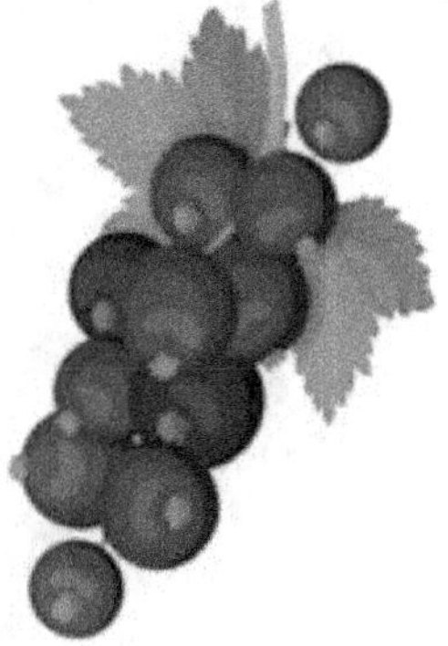

The blackcurrants are yummy.

myrtille

بلیو بیری

The blueberries are sweet.

cerise

چیری

The cherries have a stem.

noix de coco

ناریل

The coconuts have juice.

figues

انجیر

The fig has seeds.

grain de raisin

انگور

The grapes are purple.

pamplemousse

گریپ فروٹ

The grapefruits are sour.

kiwi

كيوى

The kiwi is fresh.

citron

ليموں

The lemons are yellow.

citron vert

ليموں

We have lots of lime.

litchi

ليچی

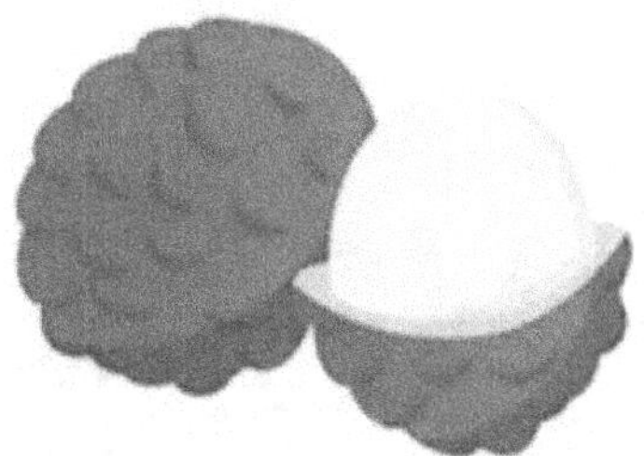

I like to eat lychee.

mandarine

مینڈارن سنتری

Oranges are refreshing.

mangue

آم

Mango is my favorite fruit.

orange

كينو

Mandarins are like oranges.

papaye

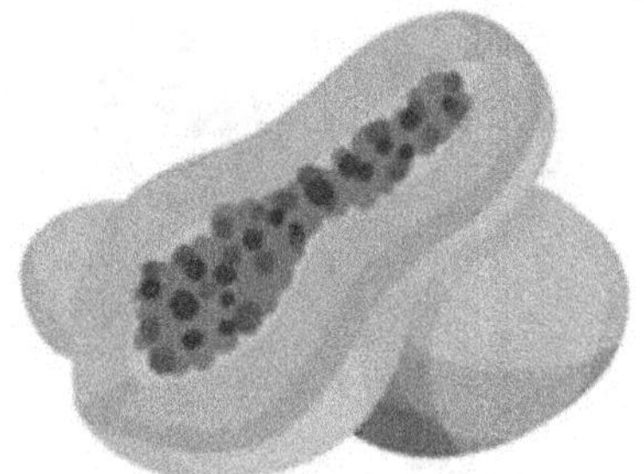

پپیتا

Papayas have lots of seeds.

pêche

آڑو

Peaches are juicy.

poire

ناشپاتی

Pears have a strange figure.

ananas

اناناس

The pineapple has a thumbs up.

prune

آلوبخاره

Plums are healthy for you.

grenade

Pomegranates are all red.

framboise

The raspberry is shiny.

fraise

The strawberry has leaves on top.

pastèque

The watermelon is big.

mandarine

The tangerine looks like an orange.

tarte

I like to eat apple pie.

gâteau

کیک

That cake is huge.

bonbons

کینڈی

Candy is not good for your teeth.

biscuit

کوکی

Cookies are easy to make.

donut

ڈونٹ

I like strawberry donuts.

crème glacée

آئس کریم

The ice cream is melting.

muffin

مفن

The muffin has a cute wrapper.

pudding

کھیر

We eat pudding on Christmas.

classeur

باندنے والا

I keep pictures in my binder.

livre

کتاب

I like to eat books.

sac à dos

بیگ

The backpack has lots of stuff.

les ciseaux

قینچی

I have scissors in my bag.

épingles

پنوں

Pins can hold stuff up.

agrafe

کلپ ویڈیو

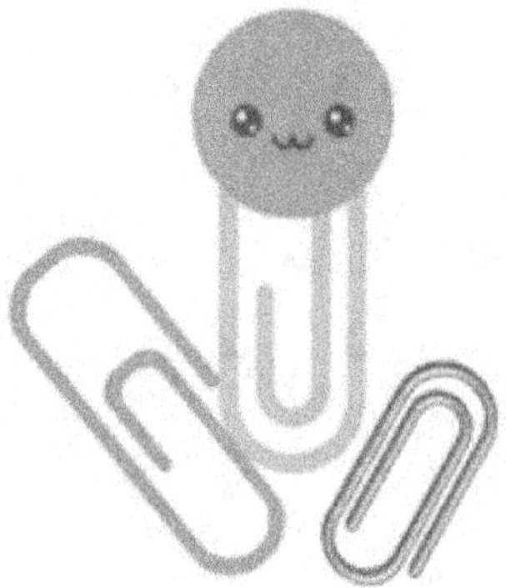

Clips can hold up paper.

papier

کاغذ

I have lots of paper.

agrafeuse

اسٹیپلر

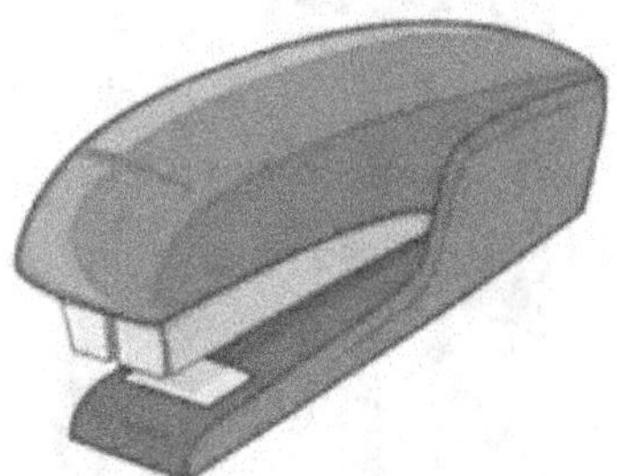

My stapler is shiny and red.

calculatrice

کیلکولیٹر

My calculator has buttons.

règle

حکمران

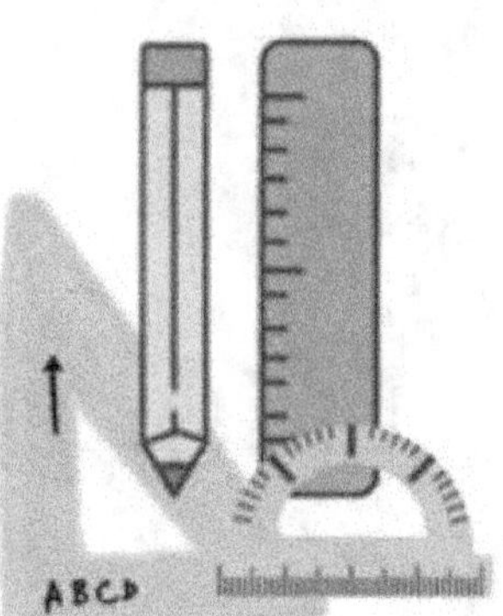

I have lots of rulers.

la colle

چپکانا

The glue is sticky.

bibliothèque

کتابوں کی الماری

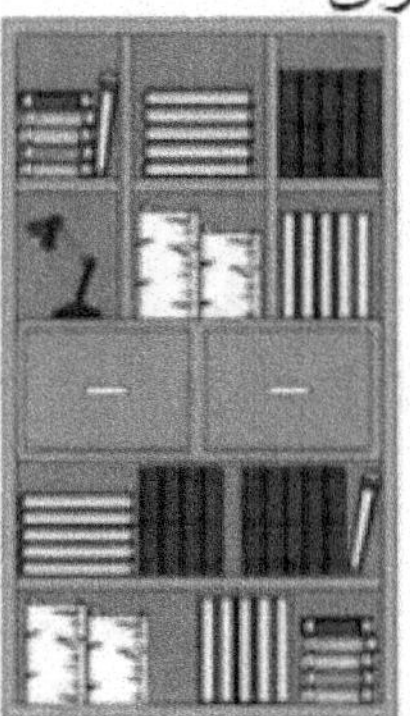

My bookcase has lots of things.

calendrier

کیلنڈر

I have a calendar on my table.

chaise

کرسی

My chair is fancy.

l'horloge

گھڑی

The clock says that it's 3 o'clock.

ordinateur

کمپیوٹر

I do things on my computer.

bureaux

ڈیسک

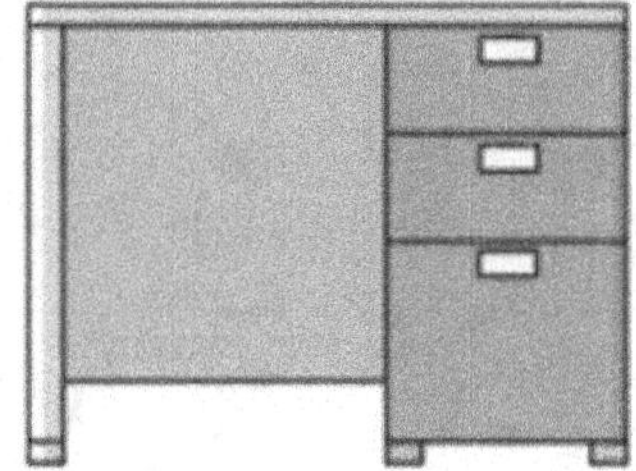

I put lots of things on my desk.

dictionnaire

لغت

The dictionary has lots of words.

la gomme

صافى

Erasers are used with pencils.

carte

نقشه

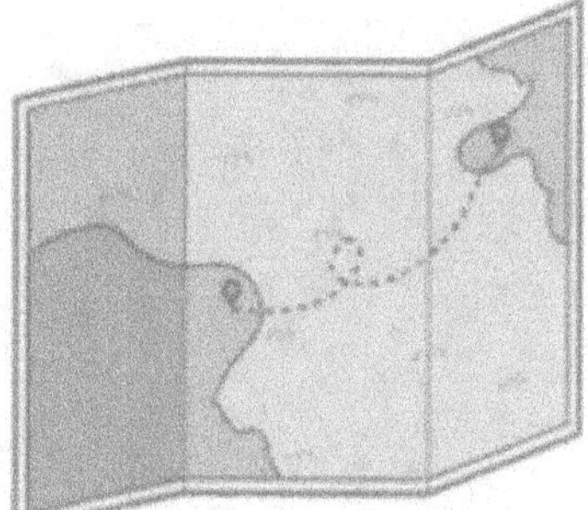

The map shows you different places.

carnet

كاپى

I use notebooks at school.

stylo

قلم

My pen is very pretty.

crayon

پينسل

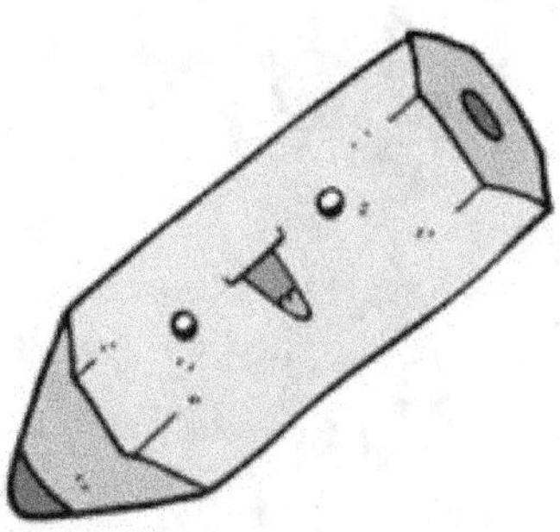

My friend gave me a pencil.

ceinture

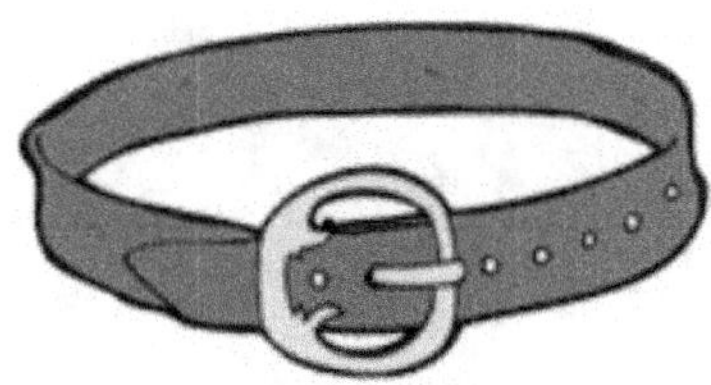

بیلٹ

I have a belt on my pants.

bottes

جوتے

I have big brown boots.

chapeau

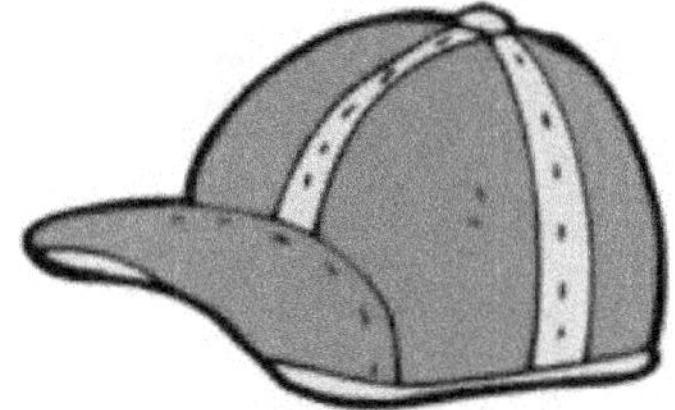

ٹوپی

My mom bought me a new cap.

manteau

کوٹ

She has a long yellow coat.

robes

کپڑے

My dress has a bow.

gants

دستانے

I got new gloves.

chapeau

ٹوپی

That hat is for a wicked witch.

veste

جیکٹ

The jacket is cozy.

jeans

جینز

My jeans are long.

pyjamas

پاجامہ

I sleep in my pajamas.

un pantalon

پتلون

The bear is wearing pants.

imperméable

برساتی

We wear our raincoats when it is raining.

écharpe

سکارف

The baby has a scarf around his neck.

chemise

قمیض

I like this shirt the best.

des chaussures

جوتے

I have red and blue shoes.

jupe

اسکرٹ

My skirt has lots of buttons.

pantalon

سلیکس

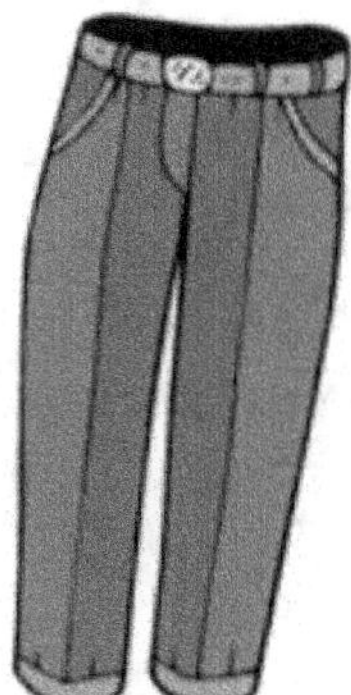

My dad wears slacks.

chaussons

چپل

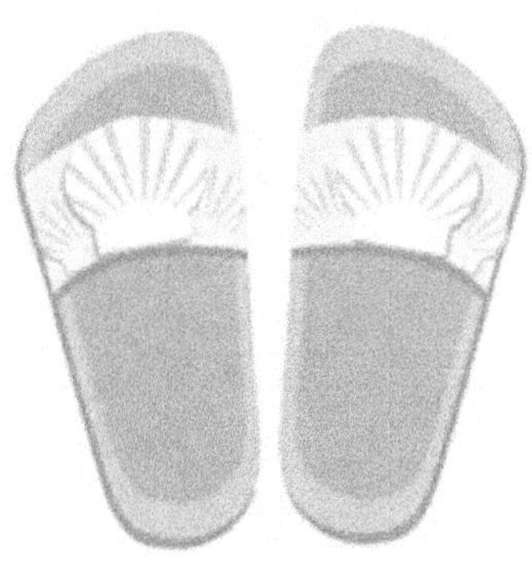

I have seashells on my sandals.

chaussettes

موزے

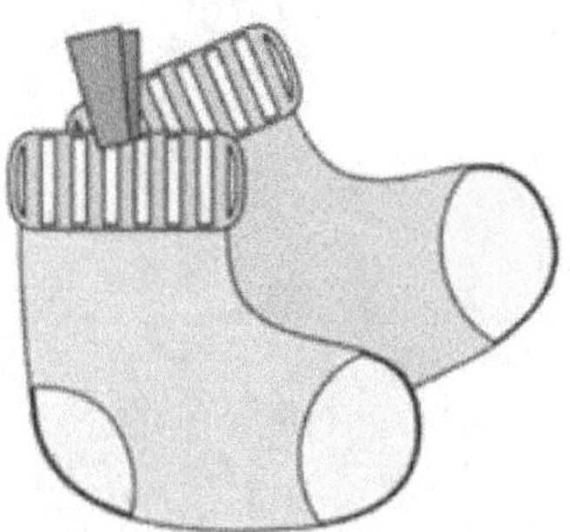

My baby sister wears socks.

costume

سوٹ

My brother is wearing a suit.

chandail

سویٹر

I am wearing a sweater for winter.

cravate

نیکٹی

My dad wears a tie to meetings.

pantalon

پتلون

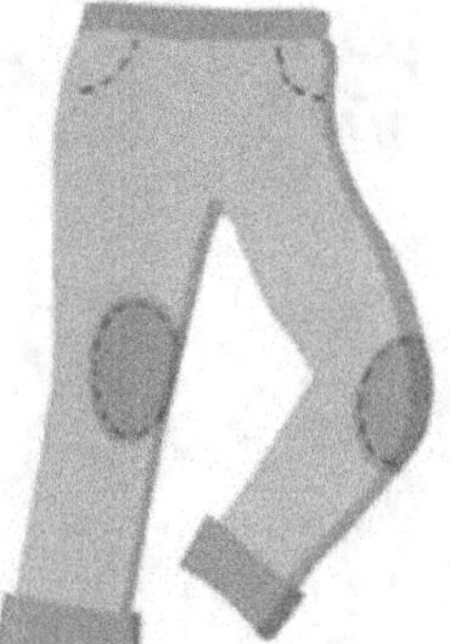

The trousers look like jeans.

slip

زیر جامہ

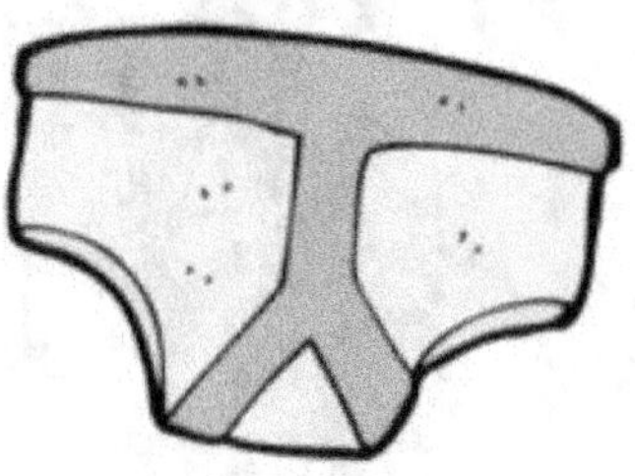

I always wear my underwear.

maillot de corps

زیر اثر

My undershirt has a star.

une

ایک

Number one and the bee are friends.

deux

دو

The cat and the mouse both love two.

trois

تین

The bear gives number three a present.

quatre

چار

Number four is a home for the cat.

cinq

پانچ

Number five hatches an egg.

six

چھ

Number six is going to eat a carrot.

sept

سات

Number seven is playing with the tiger.

huit

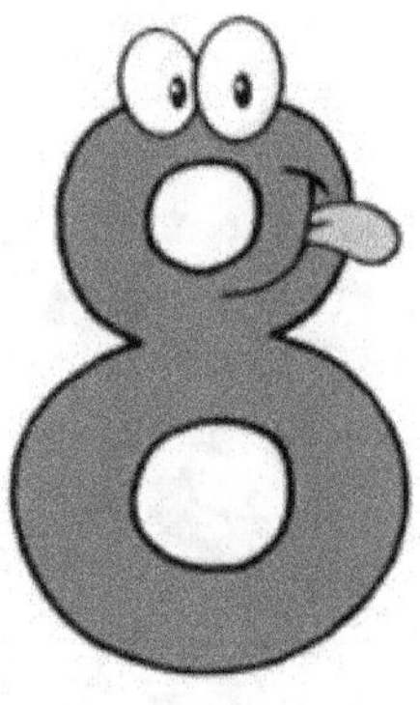

آٹھ

Number eight is funny.

neuf

نو

Number nine meets the parrot.

dix

دس

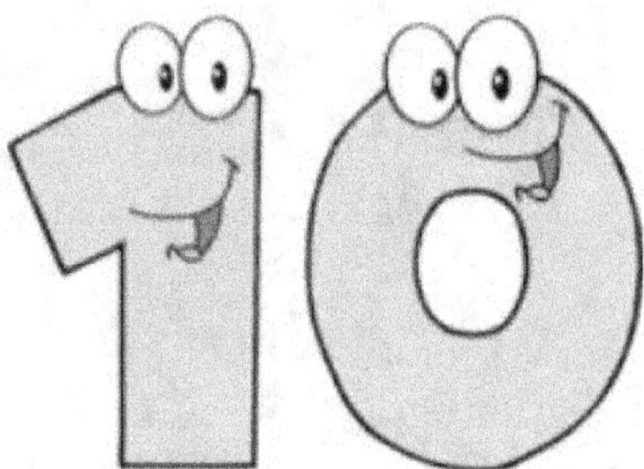

Number ten is smiling.

onze

گیارہ

Number eleven has big eyes.

douze

باره

Number twelve is number one and two.

treize

تيره

Number thirteen is excited.

quatorze

چوده

The number fourteen is vast.

quinze

پندره

The number fifteen is green.

seize

سوله

Sixteen is my lucky number.

dix-sept

ستره

Number seventeen look alike.

dix-huit

اٹھارہ

Number eighteen will go to the circus.

dix-neuf

انیس

I am nineteen now!

vingt

بیس

Number twenty has a zero.

fourmi

چیونٹی

The ant has lots of legs.

cloche

گھنٹی

The bell will ring.

vache

گائے

The cow has a bow.

poupée

گُڑیا

She has a cute bear doll.

oeuf

انڈہ

The chick has hatched out of the egg.

poisson

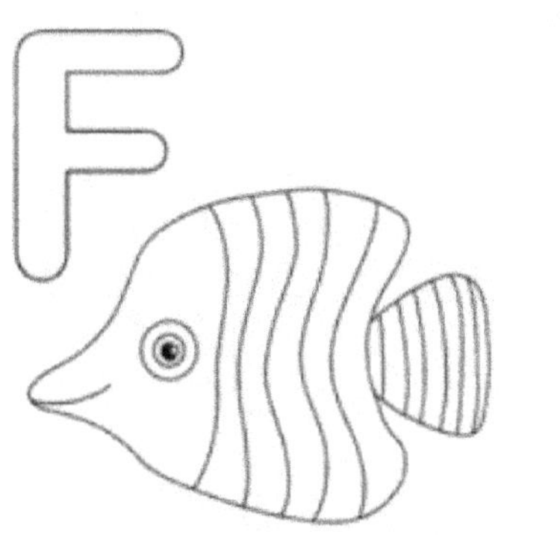

مچھلی

The fish is swimming in the water.

chèvre

بکرا

The goat is sitting on the grass.

chapeau

ٹوپی

He is wearing a hat.

crème glacée

آئس کریم

I like to eat ice cream.

confiture

جام

The kitten is sitting on the jam jar.

chaton

بلی کے بچے

The cat is sleeping on the floor.

lion

شیر

The lion is waiting for the tiger.

rat

چوہا

The mouse has lots of presents.

nez

ناک

The reindeer has a red nose.

hibou

اللو

The owl is sleeping.

porc

سور

The pig will eat cupcakes.

reine

ملکہ

The queen has a big crown.

lapin

خرگوش

The rabbit is jumping up and down.

mouton

بھیڑ

The sheep have fluffy wool.

tortue

کچھی

The turtle has a shell.

parapluie

چھتری

The mouse is holding an umbrella.

van

وین

The van is driving along the road.

pastèque

تربوز

The watermelon has lots of seeds.

xylophone

زائلفون

We are going to play the xylophone.

yaourt

دہی

We opened the yogurt can.

zèbre

زیبرا

The zebra is surprised.

rose

گلابی

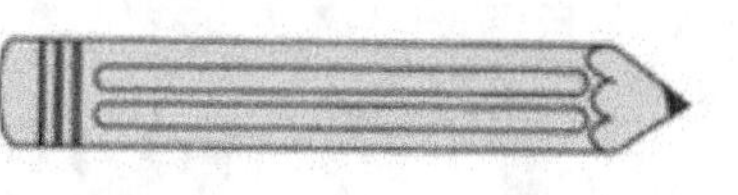

Most of my clothes are pink.

marron

برائون

color the word and
the picture in pink

brown

My chocolate is brown.

gris

سرمئی

color the word and
the picture in pink

gray

I don't like the color gray.

vert

سبز

color the word and
the picture in pink

green

The vegetables are green.

jaune

پیلا

color the word and
the picture in pink

yellow

Bananas are yellow.

blanc

سفید

color the word and
the picture in pink

white

The paper that I write on is white.

rouge

سرخ

color the word and
the picture in pink

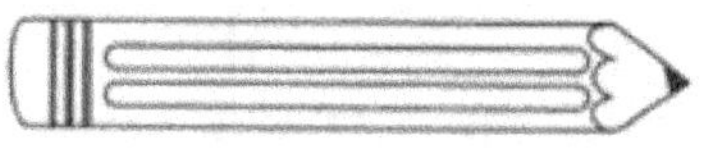

red

Apples are red.

bleu

نیلے

The night sky is blue.

percer

دِرل

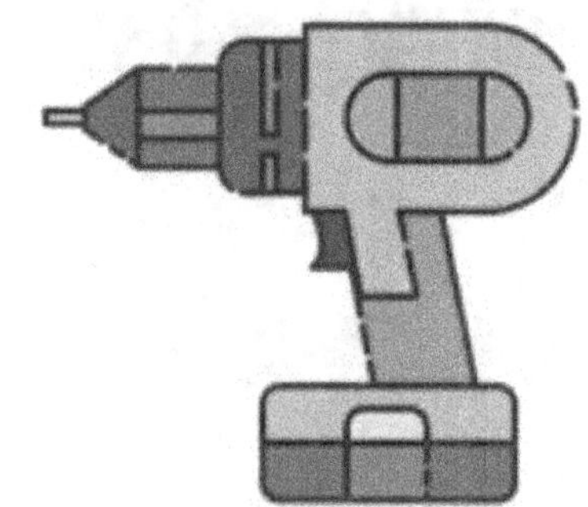

The drill will help us fix this.

marteau

بتھوڑا

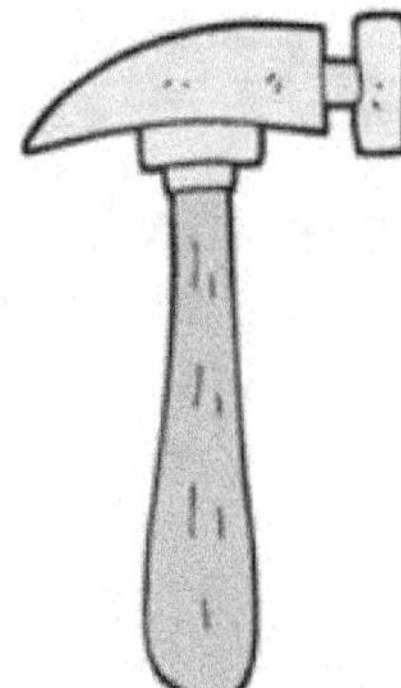

The hammer is going to nail the picture.

couteau

چاقو

The knife is sharp.

pinces

چمٹا

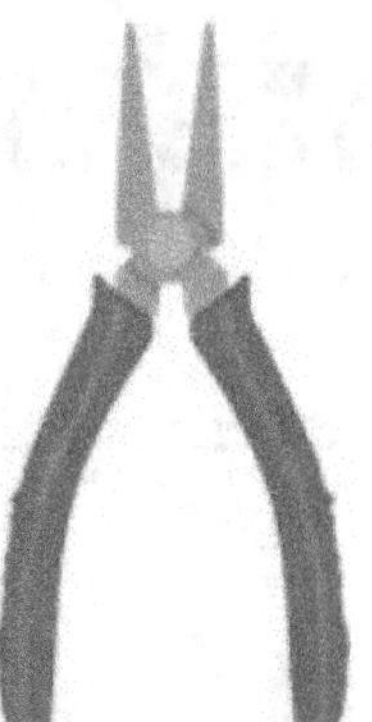

The plier is used for many things.

vu

دیکھا

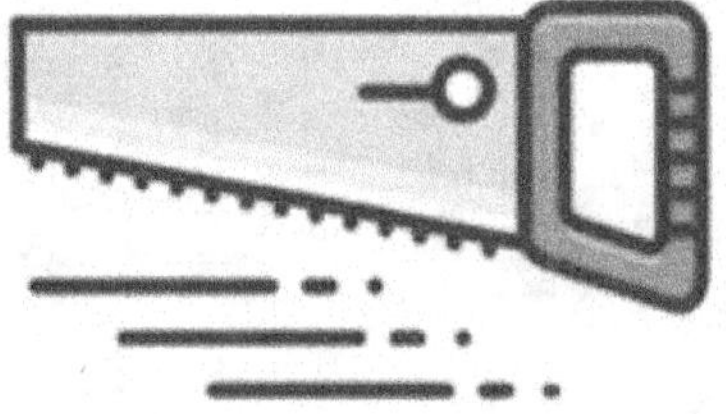

The saw can chop wood.

les ciseaux

قینچی

I use scissors to cut paper.

tournevis

سکریو ڈرایور

The screwdriver can screw in the knots.

clé

رنچ

The wrench can help unscrew the knots.

avion

ہوائی جہاز

The airplane is going to leave now.

vélo

بائیسکل

The bicycle is beautiful.

bateau

کشتی

The boat is floating on the water.

autobus

بس

The bus is going to school.

voiture

گاڑی

The car is green.

hélicoptère

ہیلی کاپٹر

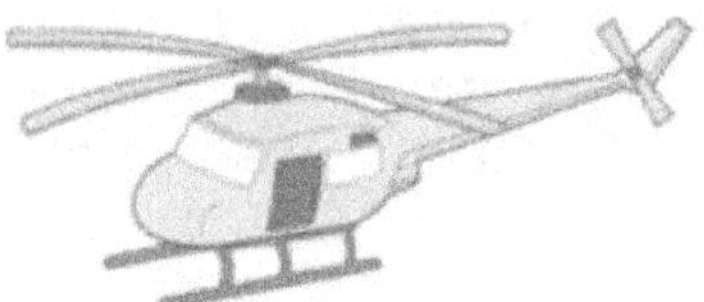

The helicopter is looking for something.

cheval

گھوڑا

You can ride the horse.

jet

جیٹ

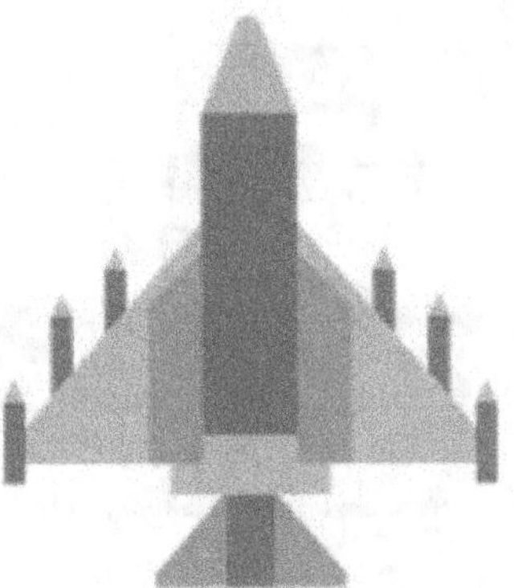

The jet is high-speed.

moto

موٹرسائیکل

The motorcycle is on the road.

navire

جہاز

The ship is on the water.

métro

سب وے

My mom goes on the subway to work.

taxi

ٹیکسی

The taxi has someone inside.

train

ٹرین

The train is going slowly.

un camion

ٹرک

The truck has stuff in it.

asperges

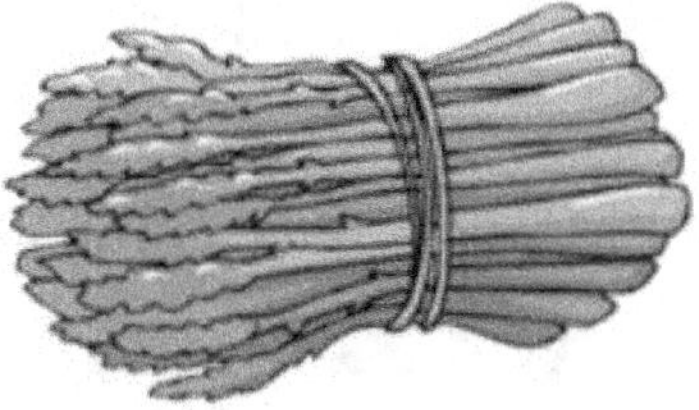

موصلی سفید

The asparagus is in a bundle.

des haricots

پھلیاں

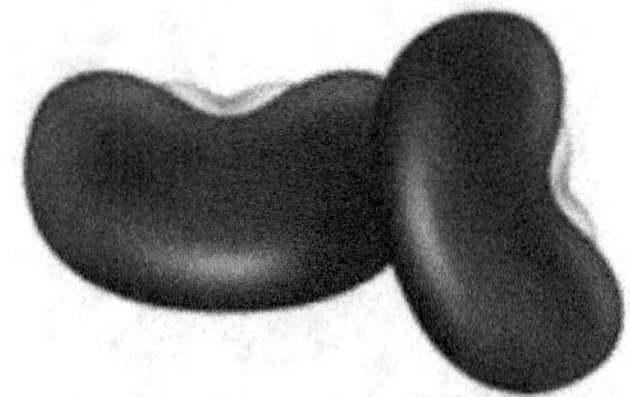

The beans are smooth.

brocoli

بروکولی

The broccoli is dancing.

chou

گوبھی

Bunnies like to eat cabbage.

carotte

گاجر

The carrots are very long.

céleri

اجوائن

The celery has lots of leaves.

blé

مکئی

Corn soup is delicious.

concombre

کھیرا

The cucumbers are cut into pieces.

aubergine

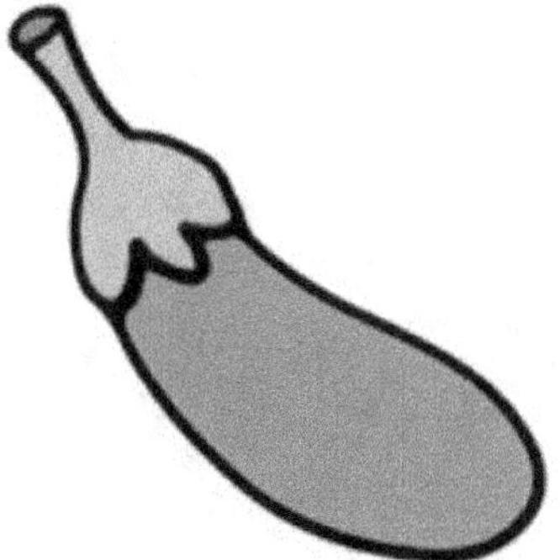

بینگن

The eggplant is purple.

poivre vert

سبز مرچ

The green pepper is juicy.

salade

لیٹس

The lettuce is all green.

oignon

پیاز

The onions make my eyes water.

pois

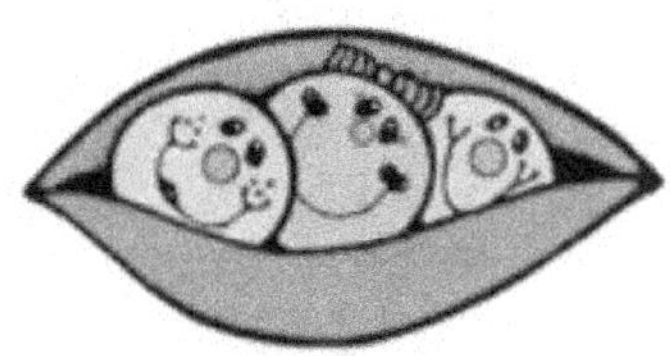

مٹر

The peas are all in a pod.

patate

آلو

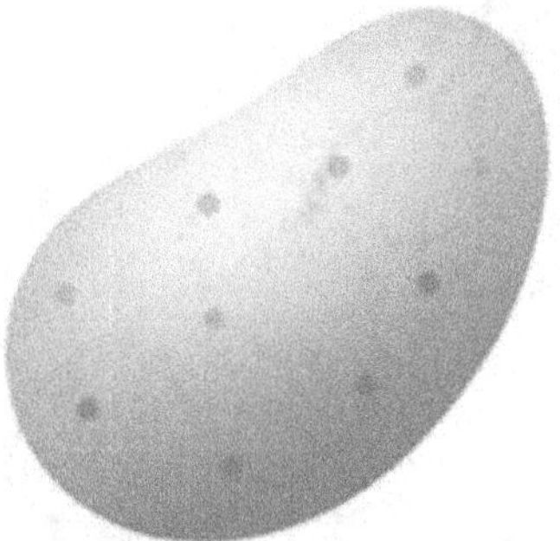

The potato is very shiny.

citrouille

قددو

The pumpkin is for Halloween.

un radis

راشد

The radish is a type of vegetable.

épinard

پالک

The spinach is good with cheese.

patate douce

شکر قندی

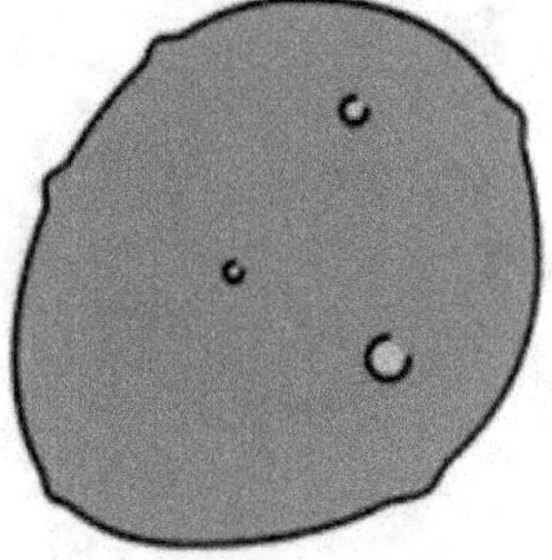

The sweet potato is quite sweet.

tomate

ٹماٹر

I don't like to eat tomatoes.

navet

شلجم

My mom bought some turnips.

nuageux

ابر آلود

The weather is cloudy today.

du froid

سردی

I like cold weather.

cool

ٹھنڈا

The temperature is cold today.

brumeux

دھند

The fog is so strong I can't see the city.

chaud

گرم

The fire is burning hot.

humide

مرطوب

It's so humid and wet today.

pluvieux

بارش

It's raining very hard.

neigeux

برفیلی

Welcome to snow land!

orageux

طوفانی

I hate the stormy weather.

ensoleillé

دھوپ

The sun is shining!

chaud

گرم

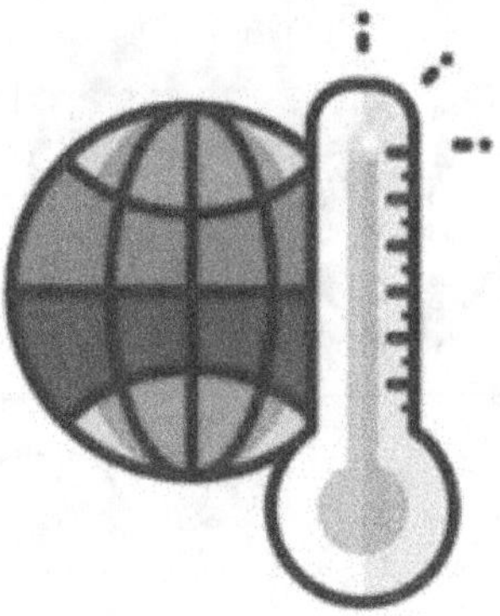

The whole world is warm today!

venteux

تیز ہوا

The leaves are blowing away since it's so windy!

tante

خالہ

My aunt is very nice to me.

frère

بھائی

My brother is very fun to play with.

cousin

کزن

I love going to the playground with my cousin.

fille

بیٹی

I like to read books with my daughter.

père

باپ

My father is playing with me.

petite fille

پوتی

My granddaughter has blond hair.

grand-mère

دادی

My grandmother is very old and has glasses.

petit fils

پوتا

My grandson and I are very excited today!

mère

ماں

My mother likes to pick me up.

neveu

بھتیجے

My father's nephew is my cousin.

nièce

بھتیجی

My niece is very good at playing ball.

sœur

بہن

My sister is so pretty!

fils

بیٹا

My son likes to play with toy cars.

belle fille

سوتیلی بیٹی

My stepdaughter likes the color orange.

belle-mère

سوتیلی ماں

My stepmother is pretty.

beau-fils

stepson

This is my stepson, Greg.

oncle

چچا

My uncle tells lots of funny jokes.

bol

پیالہ

The bowl has nothing inside.

tasse

کپ

My mom drinks her coffee out of a cup.

plat

ڈِش

That dish has a bone inside.

fourchette

کانٹا

We have more spoons than forks.

verre

گلاس

I have a glass of water on my desk.

couteau

چاقو

I have a knife in my kitchen.

agresser

پیالا

This mug of coffee is for my dad.

serviette de table

رومال

You can use the napkins to clean your hands.

poivre

کالی مرچ

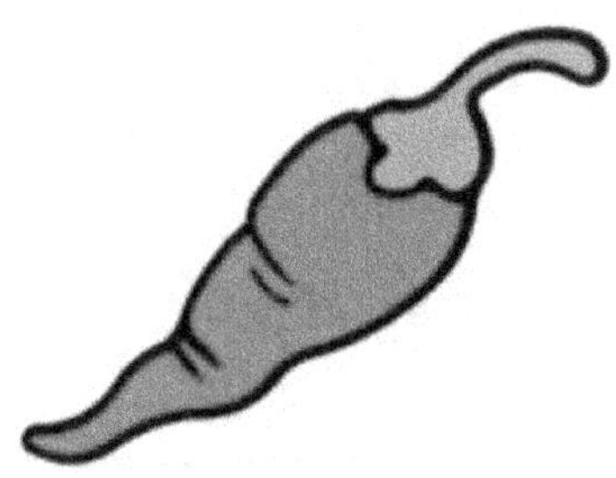

The pepper is very spicy.

lanceur

گھڑا

Pour yourself some lemonade from the pitcher.

assiette

پلیٹ

Can you help me wash the plates?

salade

سلاد

The salad is very healthy for you.

sel

نمک

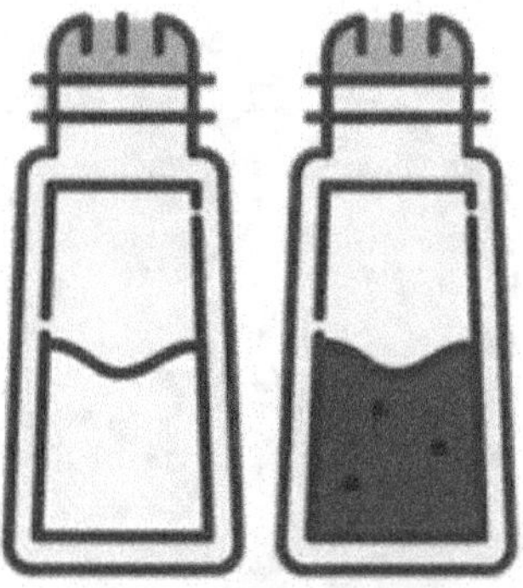

The salt tastes good with a few pinches of pepper.

soucoupe

طشتری

The plate is for my cup.

cuillère

چمچ

I use a spoon to eat my rice.

sucre

شکر

The pack of sugar is very heavy.

dimanche

اتوار

Sunday

Sunday is the day to go to Church!

lundi

پیر

Monday

Monday is the day to start school.

mardi

منگل

Tuesday

We will go to the shops on Tuesday.

mercredi

بدھ

Wednesday

Wednesday is hard to spell!

jeudi

جمعرات

Thursday

Thursday is the fourth day of the week!

vendredi

جمعہ

Friday

My birthday is on Friday!

samedi

ہفتہ

Saturday

Saturday is the weekend!

cuire

بناو

The chef will bake a cake.

ébullition

ابالنا

I will boil the eggs.

griller

برائل

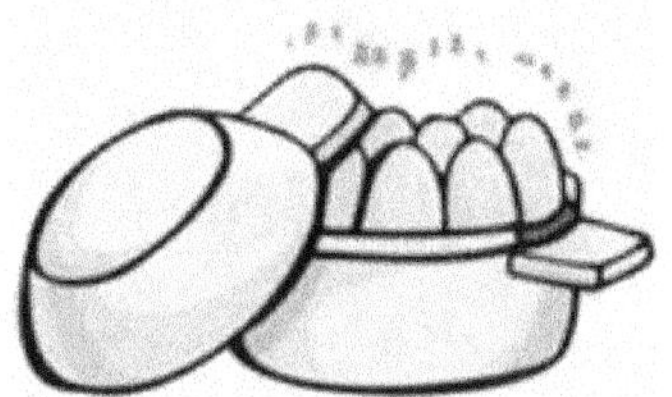

Broil is very yummy.

ouvre-boîte

اوپنر کر سکتے ہیں

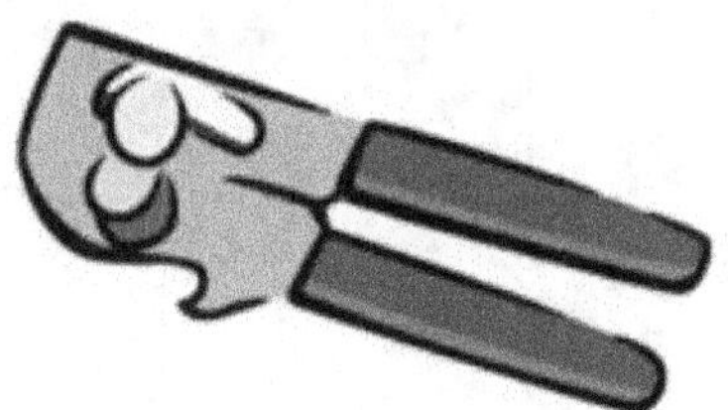

That can opener is used for
opening cans.

frire

بھون

The pan can fry lots of things.

gril

گرل

We have a grill in our backyard.

tasse à mesurer

ماپنے کا کپ

My mom uses the measuring cup
for baking.

cuillère à mesurer

ماپنے کا چمچ

I use a measuring spoon to eat my dessert.

four micro onde

مائکروویو

The microwave is used to heat food.

bol à mélanger

اختلاط کٹورا

She is using the mixing bowl to mix things.

serviettes en papier

کاغذ کے تولیے

Dry your hands with paper towels.

poché aux œufs

انڈے کی تیلی

The poach is put on noodles.

porte pot

برتن ہولڈر

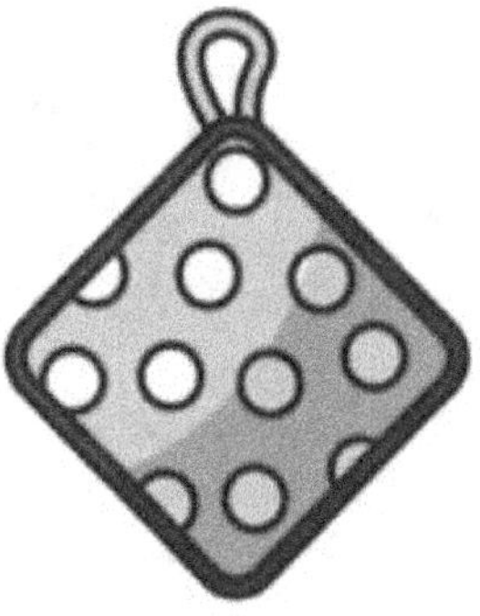

The potholder is soft.

rôti

روسٹ

The chef made roast chicken.

rouleau à pâtisserie

بیلن

He is holding a rolling pin.

brouiller

جدوجہد

My mom is making scrambled
eggs for breakfast.

mijoter

النابا

The simmer is rice today.

couteau

چاقو

The knife is sharp.

cuillère

چمچ

I eat my food with a spoon and
fork.

spatule

spatula

The spatula will help us flip the steak over.

vapeur

بھاپ

The steam is coming from the pot.

passoire

دباؤ

The strainer is used to strain stuff.

minuteur

ٹائمر

I set my timer for 12:00.

fourchette

کانٹا

I have lots of metallic forks.

grille-pain

ٹوسٹر

The toaster will toast my bread.

bouilloire

كيتلی

The kettle has tea inside.

réfrigérateur

ریفریجریٹر

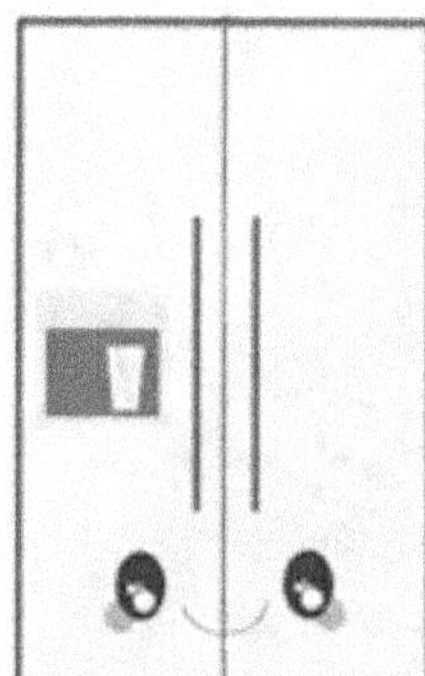

The refrigerator has lots of things inside.

mixeur

بلینڈر

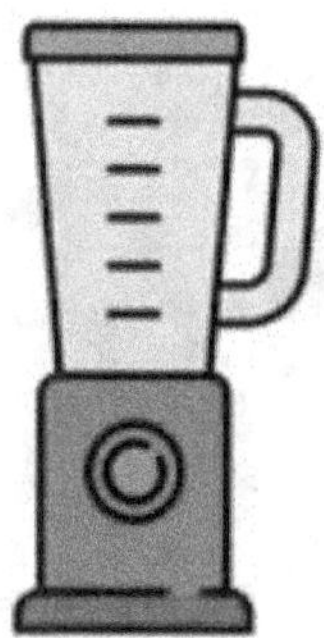

The blender will mix up my fruits.

cabinets

کیبینٹ

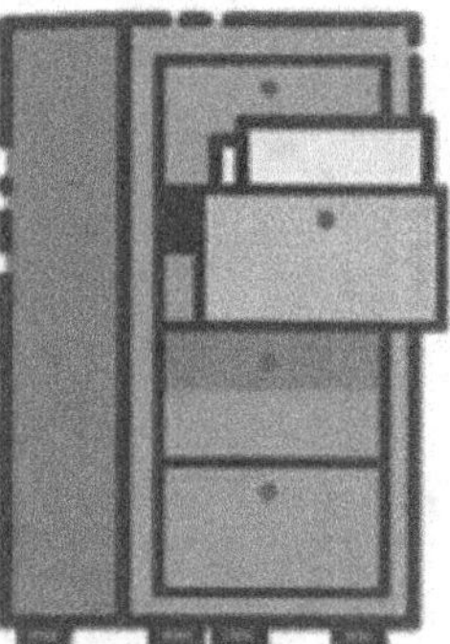

The cabinet has my paper inside.

placard

الماری

The cupboard has lots of books.

four micro onde

مائکروویو

The microwave will heat my food.

arrière

پیچھے

She has a slender back.

des joues

گال

She kisses her mom on the cheek.

poitrine

سینے

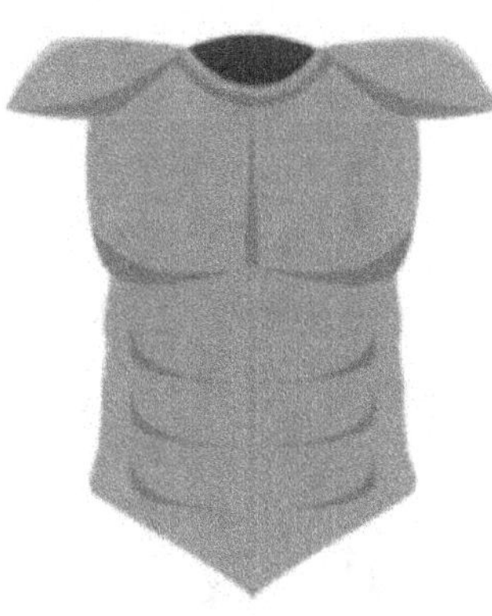

The armor is for your chest.

menton

ٹھوڑی

This is my chin!

oreilles

کان

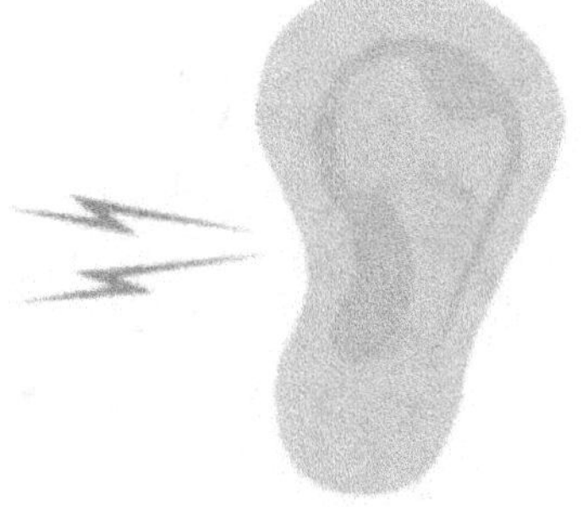

The ear is hearing something.

les sourcils

ابرو

The eyebrows are raised.

yeux

آنکھیں

The eyes are blue.

pieds

پاؤں

I have one pair of feet.

des doigts

انگلیاں

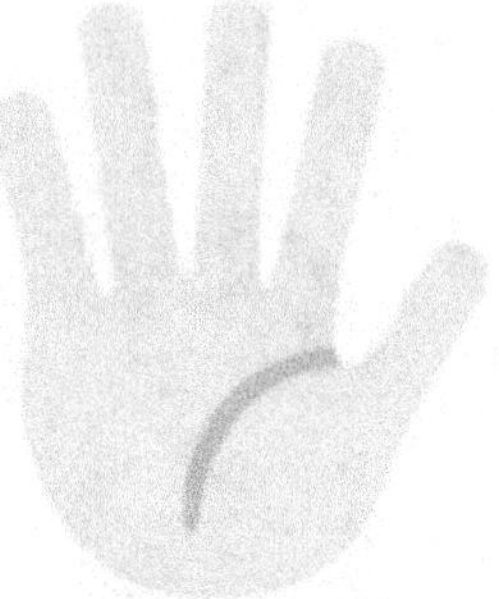

The fingers are waving at us.

pied

پاؤں

My foot has five fingers.

front

پیشانی

My brain is behind my forehead.

cheveux

بال

My hair is long and black.

mains

باتھ

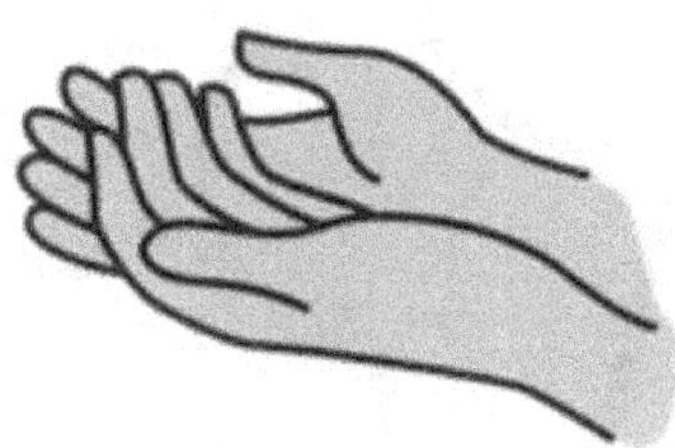

I will wash my hands in the sink.

tête

سر

She has a big head.

les hanches

کولہوں

The gorilla has his hands on his hips.

les genoux

گھٹنوں

She is begging on her knees.

jambes

ٹانگوں

The tiger has strong legs.

lèvres

ہونٹ

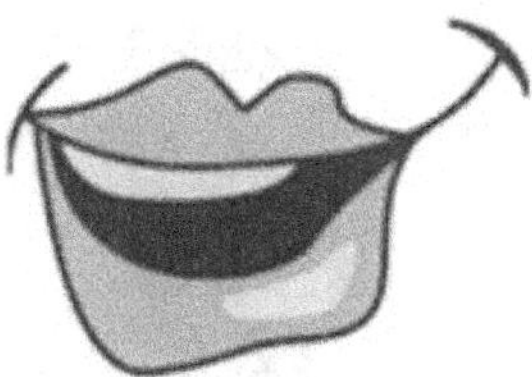

The lips have lipstick on.

bouche

منہ

He is covering his mouth with his hand.

cou

گردن

The necklace is very special to me.

nez

ناک

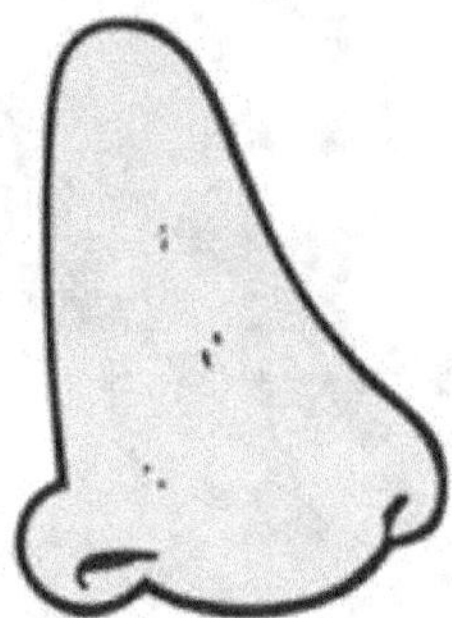

The nose smells something.

épaules

کندھوں

He puts his hands on his shoulders.

estomac

پیٹ

He has a big stomach.

les dents

دانت

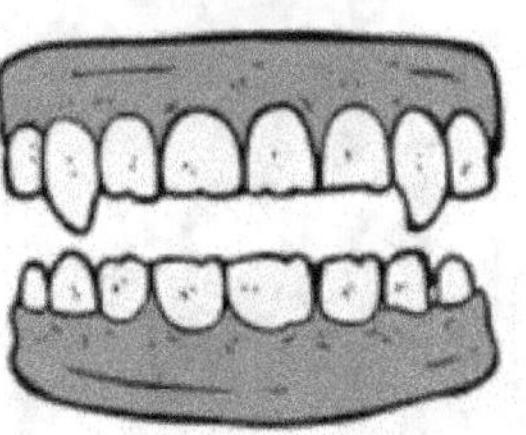

The teeth are clean and white.

gorge

حلق

He has a sore throat today.

les orteils

انگلیوں

My toes are small.

langue

زبان

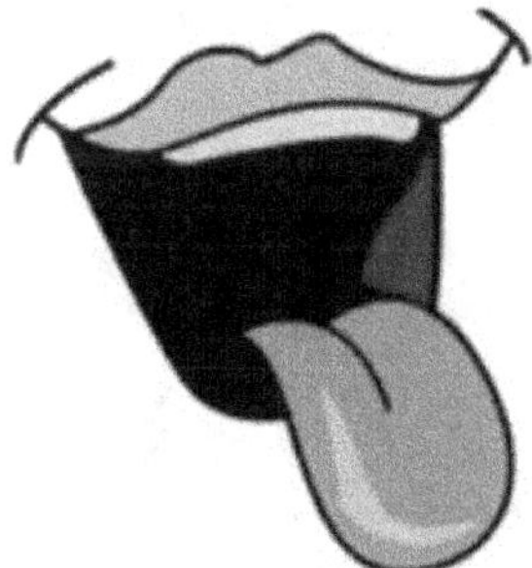

My tongue is licking ice cream.

dent

دانت

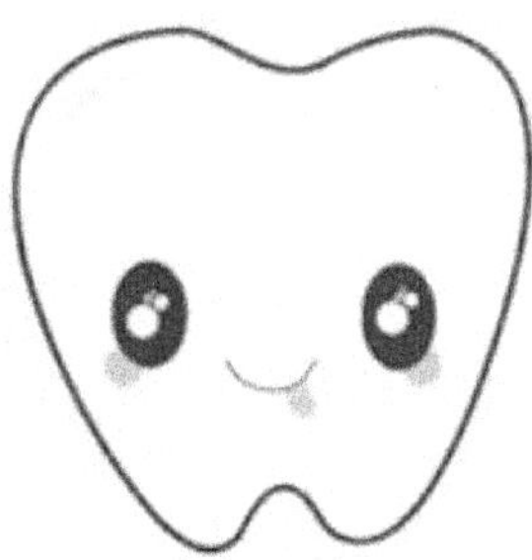

The tooth has big eyes.

taille

کمر

He has his hands on his waist.

salopette

overalls کے

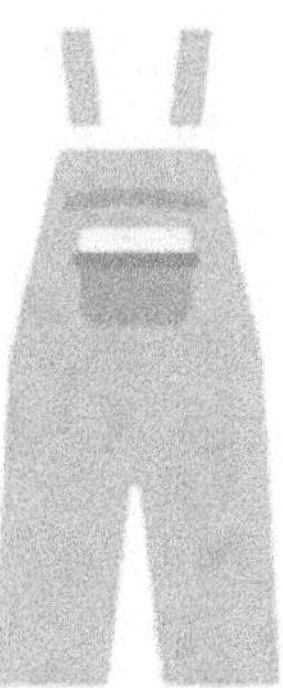

I bought these overalls for you!

mitaines

گھٹّا دینا

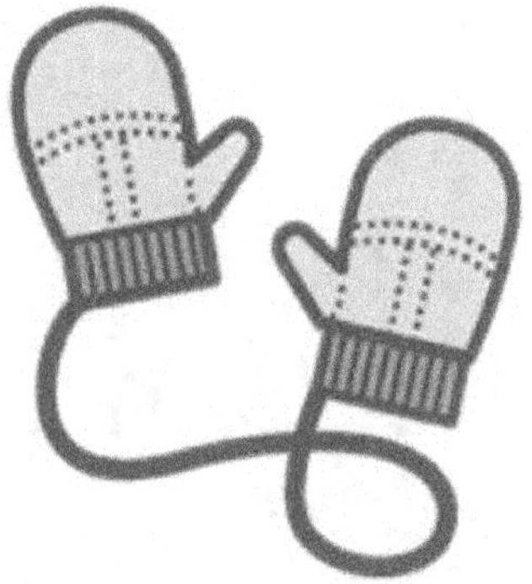

The mittens are very warm.

bonnet

بیانی

The beanie is for winter.

tablier

تہبند

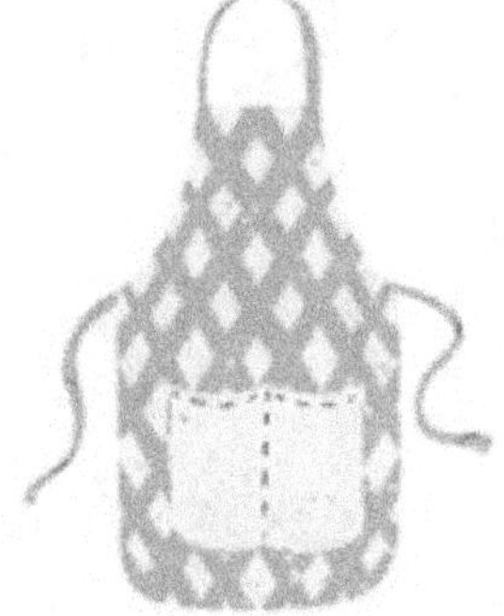

I wear my apron when I bake.

poupée

گڑیا

The doll is for my baby sister.

hochets

جھگڑے

The rattle is for the baby.

jouet

کھلونا

The toy is very fun.

couche

ڈایپر

The baby has to wear a diaper.

berceau

باسینیٹ

She is sleeping in her bassinet.

bavoir

بی بی

My baby brother has to wear his
bib when he is eating.

octogone

آکٹگون

The octagon is saying okay!

triangle

مثلث

The triangle has three corners.

carré

مربع

Square

The square has four sides.

cercle

دائره

Circle

The circle is round.

ovale

اوول

The oval shape looks like a circle.

cœur

دل

I drew a heart on my paper.

traverser

كراس

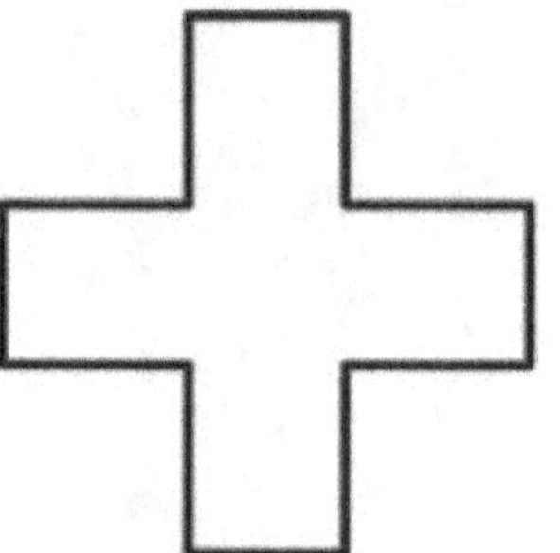

That sign is a cross.

la flèche

يرو

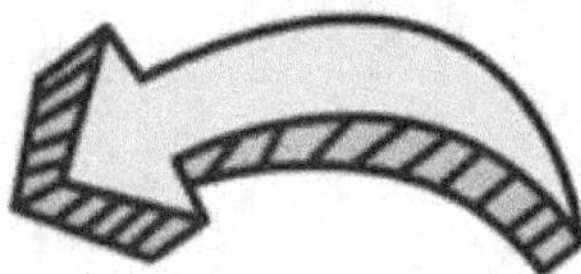

The arrow is pointing this way.

cube

مكعب

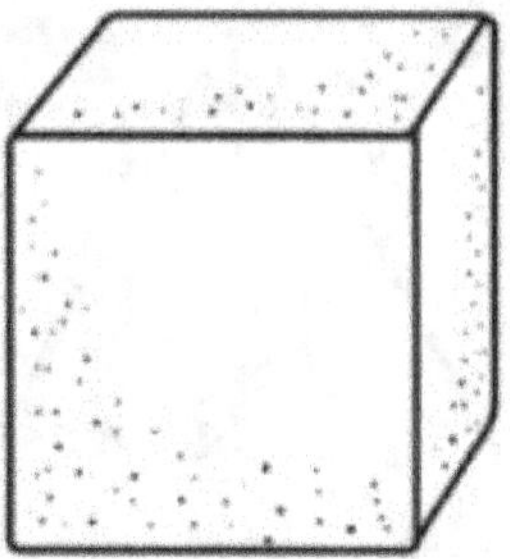

The cube is 3D.

étoile

ستاره

The star is yellow and shiny.

tir à l'arc

تیر اندازی

The archery is where you aim.

badminton

بیڈمنٹن

My favorite sport is badminton.

criquet

کرکٹ

I am very good at cricket.

bowling

بولنگ

I got one pin down at bowling!

boxe

باکسنگ

The boxing gloves are hot.

tennis

تینس

He can hit the ball in tennis.

faire de la planche a roulettes

اسکیٹ بورڈنگ

He skateboards to school.

planche de surf

سرفبورڈنگ

The shark loves surfing in the ocean.

le hockey

ہاکی

I like to play Ice hockey.

yoga

یوگا

He is closing his eyes and doing yoga.

épée

تلوار پلے

They are fencing and dueling together.

aptitude

صحت

She will do some fitness in the pool.

gymnastique

جمناسٹکس

He can do brilliant gymnastics.

karaté

کراٹے

She is good at kicking in Karate.

volley-ball

والی بال

She is holding a volleyball.

musculation

ویٹ لفٹنگ

The girl with brown hair can do weightlifting.

basketball

باسکٹ بال

He can balance the ball with one finger in basketball.

base-ball

بیس بال

The little chick is in the finales at baseball.

le rugby

رگبی

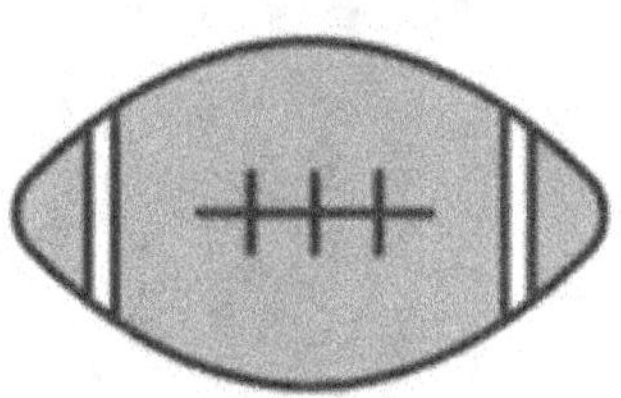

The rugby ball has white stripes.

lutte

کشتی

The sumo will compete in wrestling.

course de voitures

کار ریسنگ

He is number one for car racing.

cyclisme

سائیکلنگ

He is peacefully cycling on the road.

fonctionnement

چل رہا ہے

He is running while listening to his earphones.

tennis de table

ٹیبل ٹینس

My brother and dad will play table tennis.

pêche

ماہی گیری

He will go to the river to fish.

judo

جوڈو

She has a red belt in Judo.

escalade

چڑھنا

He will climb the ladder.

tournage

شوٹنگ

He is shooting the archery board.

le golf

گولف

She is going to compete in the golf competition.

balade

سواری

He will ride his scooter.

asseyez-vous

بیٹھ جاؤ

They are sitting down together.

se lever

کھڑے ہوجاؤ

She likes to stand up.

bats toi

لڑو

They are fighting over the book.

rire

ہنسنا

He is laughing so hard!

lis

پڑھیں

She read a picture book.

jouer

كھیلیں

He went to play on the slide.

ecoutez

سنو

He listened for the ice cream cart.

pleurer

رونا

He cried because he got a bad grade.

pense

سوچو

He thought that the test would be hard.

chanter

گانا

He sang for the concert.

regarder la télévision

ٹی وی دیکھو

He watched TV the whole night.

danse

رقص

She was a good dancer.

allumer

آن کر دو

The light is turned on.

éteindre

بند کریں

The light is turned off.

gagner

جیت

He won the contest.

mouche

اڑنا

The parrot can fly.

couper

کٹ

He was cutting his nails.

désinvolte

پھینک دو

He threw away the garbage.

dormir

سوئے

He slept soundly.

fermer

بند کریں

He closed his mouth shut.

ouvert

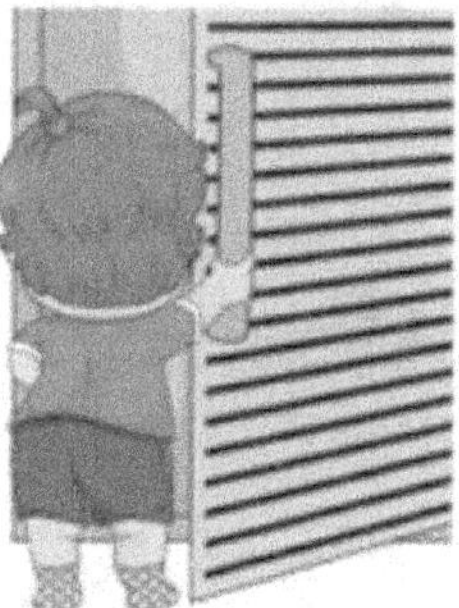

کھولو

She opened the bathroom door.

écrire

لکھیں

She wrote with a pencil.

donner

دے دو

Santa gave her a present.

sauter

چھلانگ لگائیں

She had fun jumping.

manger

کھاؤ

The shark ate yummy ice cream.

boisson

پیو

The old British man drank tea.

cuisinier

کک

The microwave cooked his soup.

lavage

دھوئے

You need to remember to wash
your hands.

attendre

رکو

He was waiting for the bus.

montée

چڑھنا

She climbed a lot of mountains.

parler

بات کریں

Two best friends were talking together.

crawl

رینگنا

The baby crawled on the floor.

rêver

خواب

The Sloth dreamed about eating leaves.

creuser

کھودو

That strong man dug a swimming pool.

taper

تالیاں بجانا

The baby clapped her hands.

tricoter

بننا

She knits with the purple string.

coudre

سلائی

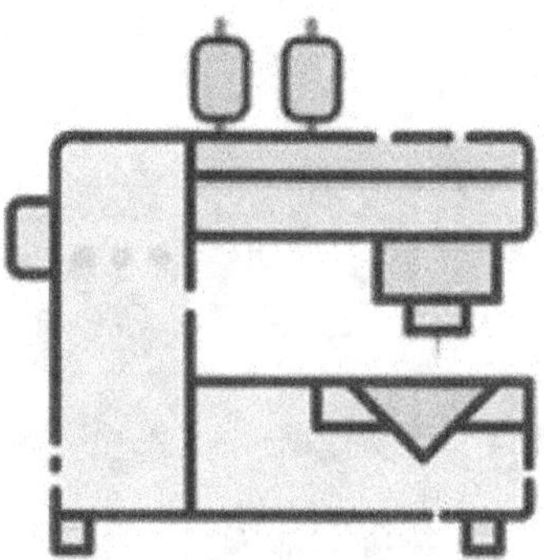

That is a sewing machine.

odeur

بو آ رہی ہے

The perfume smelled great.

baiser

چومنا

He kissed his mother.

étreinte

گلے

They hugged each other.

ronfler

خراٹے

The tiger snored.

baigner

غسل دینا

He took a bath.

s'incliner

رکوع

He bowed to the judge.

peindre

پینٹ

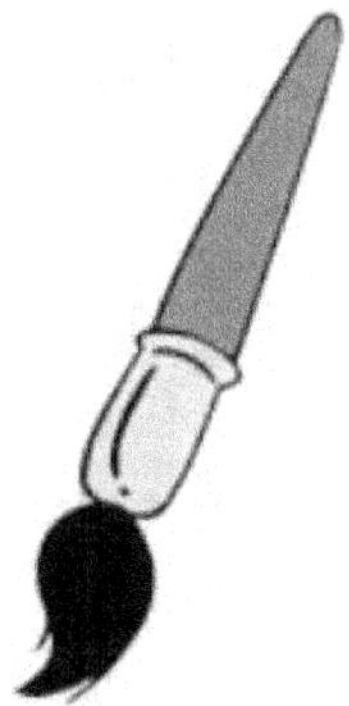

He painted a colorful picture.

se plonger

ڈوبکی

He dove to the deepest part of the ocean.

ski

اسکی

The ski was expensive.

empiler

اسٹیک

The books are stacked high.

acheter

خریدنے

They bought cereal.

secouer

ہلائیں

They shook hands together.

programmeur

پروگرامر

He was a smart computer programmer.

vétérinaire

جانوروں سے چلنے والا

She is a veterinarian.

vendeur de rue

پھیری والے

That street vendor sells hot dogs.

mineur

کان کن

That Miner will find gold.

prof

استاد

The owl is the teacher.

groom

بیل بوائے

That Bellboy is fat.

orateur

اسپیکر

The chicken is a great Speaker.

boucher

کسائ

The Butcher sells fish.

pharmacien

فارماسسٹ

That Pharmacist saved a person's life.

réceptionniste

استقبالیہ

He is a Receptionist.

politicien

سیاستدان

He wants to be a Politician.

guide touristique

ٹُور گائیڈؔ

That Tour guide led us around Japan.

entrepreneur

کاروباری

He is an Entrepreneur.

danseuse de ballet

بیلے ڈانسر

She is training to be a Ballet dancer.

astronaute

خلاباز

He is a great astronaut.

juge

جج

That Judge is always fair.

avocat

وكيل

The lawyer is serious.

la caissière

كيشيئر

She is a cashier at the market.

conducteur de taxi

ٹیکسی ڈرائیور

He is a fast Taxi driver.

plombier

پلمبر

That Plumber fixes toilets.

musicien

موسیقار

She wants to be a Musician like
her teacher.

chef

شیف

The chef makes fast food.

boulanger

بیکر

That baker is a bread.

artiste

آرٹسٹ

That Artist came from Italy.

acteur

اداکار

That actor is famous.

barman

بارپر

The Bartender works in a bar.

coiffeur

نائی

That girl is a Hairdresser.

évêques

بشپ

He is a Bishop.

opticien

آپٹیشین

She went to an Optician.

fleuriste

پھول والا

She is a great Florist.

écrivain

لکھاری

He is a famous author.

comptable

اکاؤنٹنٹ

My accountant is loyal.

du vin

شراب

That wine tastes good.

café

کافی

That coffee is bitter.

limonade

لیمونیڈ

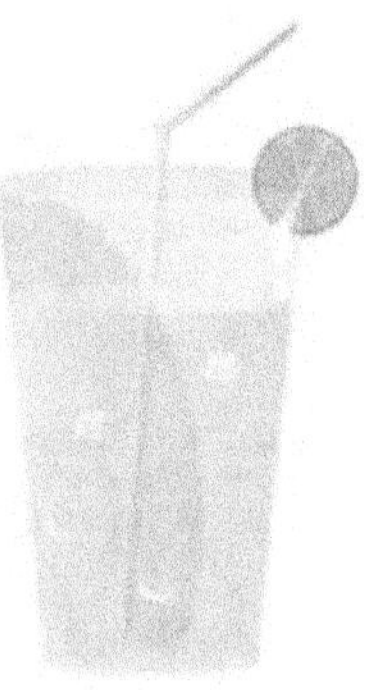

The lemonade is refreshing.

chocolat chaud

ہاٹ چاکلیٹ

I drink hot chocolate every day.

milk-shake

ملک شیک

The milkshake has whipped cream.

eau

پانی

The water is not cold.

thé

چائے

The tea is hot.

lait

دودھ

Milk is white.

bière

بیئر

The beer is foamy.

un soda

سوڈا

The soda is fizzy.

smoothie

بموار

The smoothie is a watermelon flavor.

milk-shake

ملک شیک

The milkshake has whipped cream.

lait de coco

ناریل ملا دودھ

The coconut milk is yummy.

du jus d'orange

مالٹے کا جوس

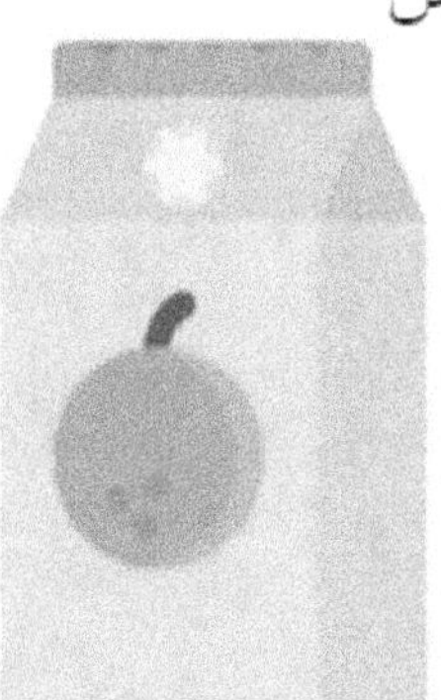

The orange juice is made from oranges.

cacao

The cocoa is sweet.

fromage

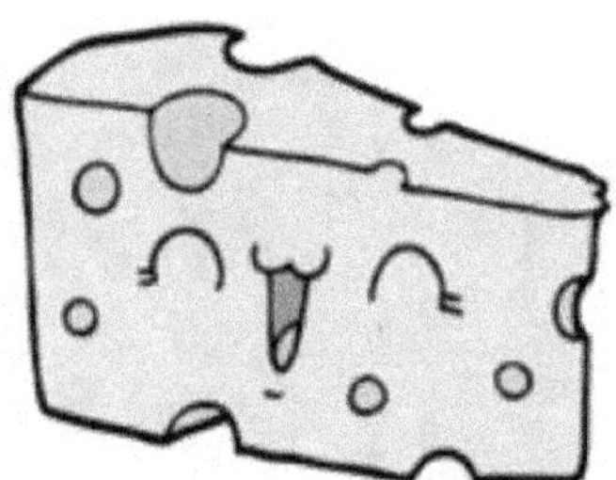

The cheese is creamy.

oeuf

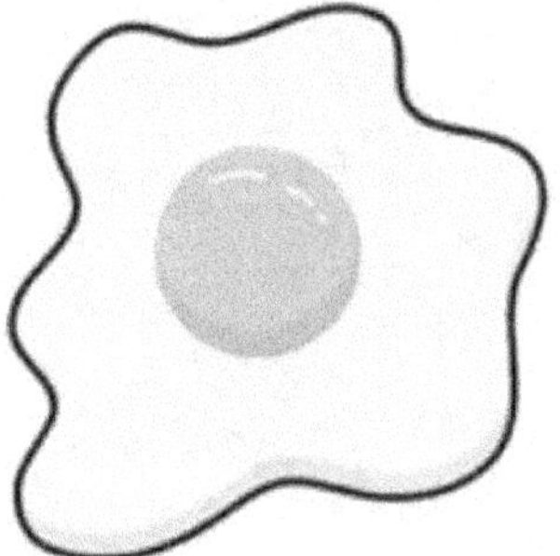

The egg is fried.

beurre

The butter is put on bread.

margarine

Margarine looks like butter.

yaourt

That yogurt is popular.

cottage cheese

پنیر

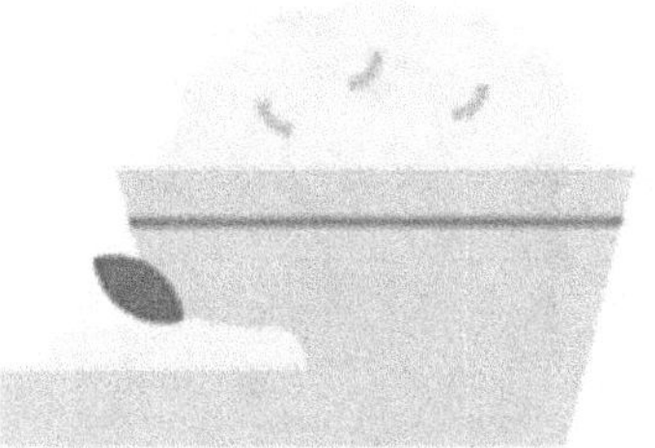

The cottage cheese is put on crackers.

crème glacée

آئس کریم

They have a triple scoop ice cream.

crème

کریم

That is a lot of creams.

sandwich

سینڈوچ

That sandwich is healthy.

saucisse

ساسیج

Americans love sausages.

hamburger

بیمبرگر

That hamburger looks happy.

hot-dog

باٹ ڈاگ

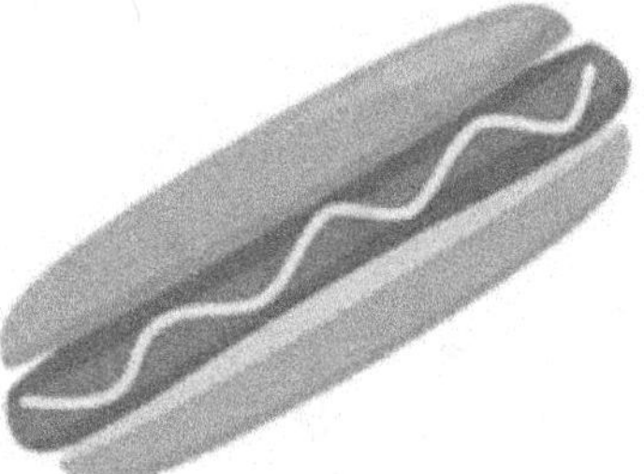

That hot dog has mustard on it.

pain

روٹی

That bread is saying hello.

pizza

پیزا

That pizza is cheesy.

steak

اسٹیک

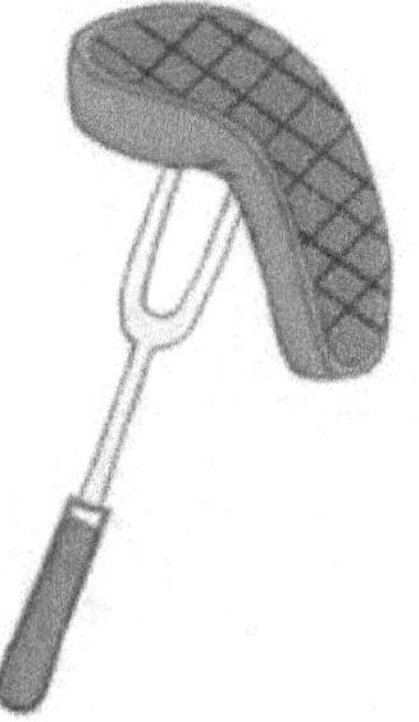

The steak was grilled.

poulet rôti

روسٹ چکن

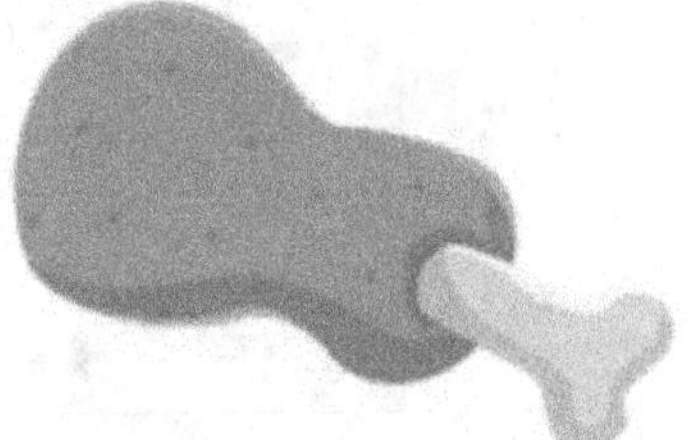

Roast Chicken is delicious.

poisson

مچھلی

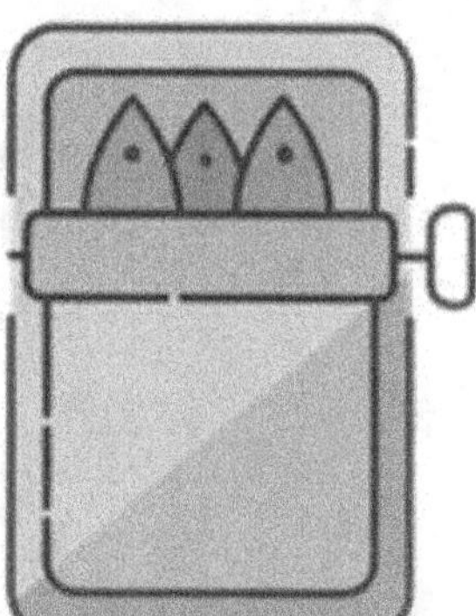

You can buy canned fish in the market.

fruit de mer

Lobster is expensive seafood.

jambon

Ham can be put in sandwiches.

kebab

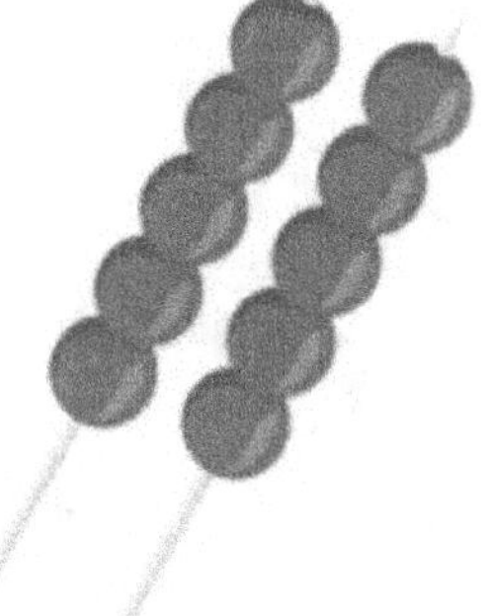

Kebab is a delicacy in America.

bacon

That bacon is smiling.

crème fraîche

You can dip your chips in sour cream.

vache

Cows are black and white.

lapin

خرگوش

That rabbit is fun to play with.

canard

بطخ

That duck is content.

crevette

کیکڑے

The shrimp has six legs.

porc

پگ

That pig is pink and fat.

abeille

مکھی

The bee has a stinger.

chèvre

بکرا

That goat has a white horn.

crabe

کیکڑے

The crab has two big pincers.

cerf

برن

That deer is sleeping.

dinde

ترکی

The turkey has a giant tail.

colombe

کبوتر

That dove is carrying a plant.

mouton

بھیڑ

That sheep has fluffy wool.

poisson

مچھلی

That fish has colorful fins.

poulet

چکن

That chicken is waking everybody up.

cheval

گھوڑا

The horse has a red mane.

chaise

کرسی

That wing chair is yellow.

meuble tv

ٹی وی اسٹینڈ

The TV stand can hold books.

canapé

صوفہ

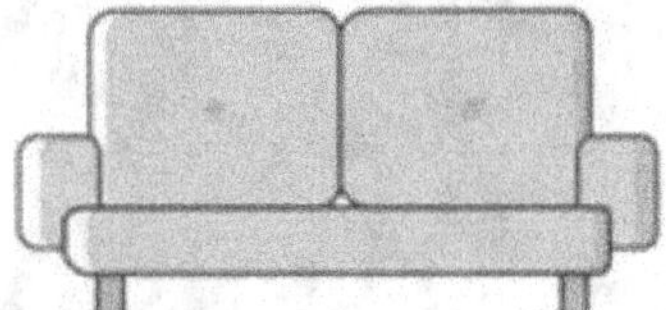

The sofa is comfortable to sit on.

coussins

کشن

The cushion helps soften your seat.

téléphone

ٹیلیفون

The telephone is ringing.

télévision

ٹیلی ویژن

That television is big.

haut-parleurs

مقررین

That speaker is used to increase the volume.

table d'appoint

سائیڈ ٹیبل

That end table is sparkling clean.

service à thé

چائے کا سیٹ

That tea set is from China.

cheminée

چمنی

The fireplace makes me warm.

télécommandes

ریموٹ

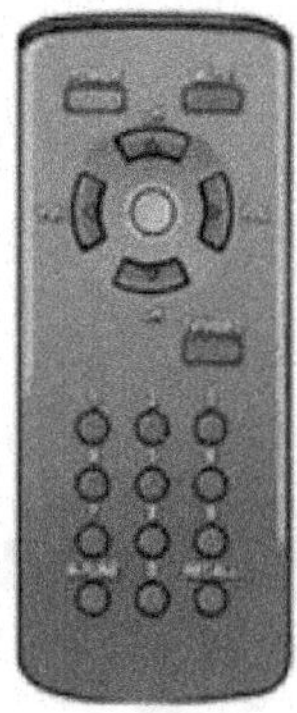

The remote has lots of buttons.

ventilateur électrique

برقی پنکھا

The fan is blowing wind.

lampadaire

فرشی لیمپ

The floor lamp is very tall.

tapis

قالین

The carpet is soft and silky.

bureaux

ڈیسک

The table is made of wood.

stores

بلائنڈز

I will pull the blinds down.

rideaux

پردے

She opened the curtains.

image

تصویر

The picture is about the mountains and the sky.

vase

گلدان

The roses are all in a vase.

l'horloge

گھڑی

The alarm clock is beeping.

oreiller

تکیہ

The pillow is pink and yellow.

cintre

ہیٹ ہینگر

The hat stand has only one hat on it.

mettre la table

سنگھار میز

I have made up on my dressing table.

lampe de table

ٹیبل لیمپ

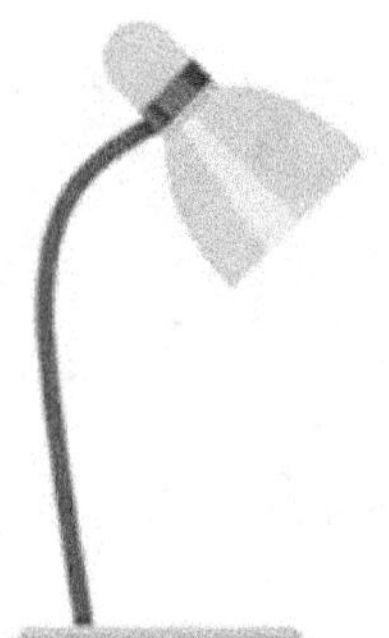

The table lamp will help me see in the dark.

miroir

آئینہ

The mirror is very tall.

planche a repasser

استری کرنے کا تختہ

Don't touch the ironing board, it's hot!

boîte avec tiroir

دراز کے ساتھ باکس

You can keep your clothes in the hope chest.

table de chevet

بستر بغل میز

The nightstand has my lamp on it.

lit

بستر

The bed is charming.

climatisation

اے سی

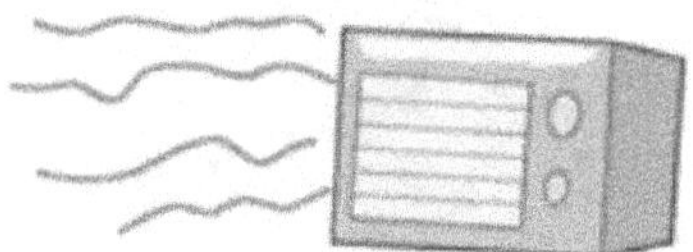

The air conditioner is cold.

cruche

جگ

The measuring jug has nothing inside.

dentifrice

دانتوں کی پیسٹ

The toothpaste is mint flavored.

brosse à dents

ٹوت برش

The toothbrush has toothpaste on it.

savon

صابن

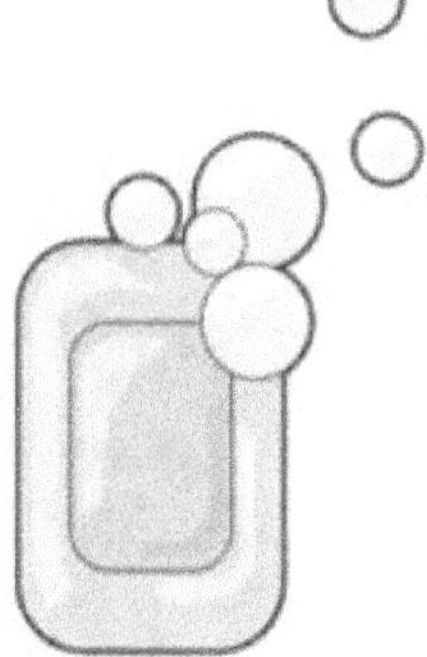

The soap is very bubbly.

pince à linge

كلاتھ اسپن

The clothespin will clip my clothes.

cintre

ہینگر

The hanger is hanging my boots.

sèche-cheveux

ہیئر ڈرائیر

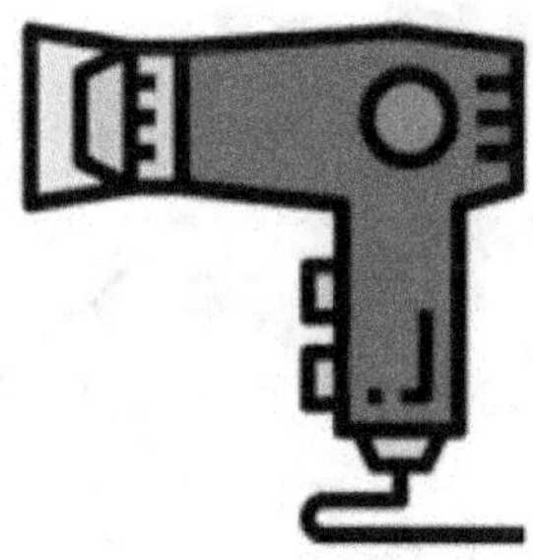

The hairdryer will blow my hair.

shampooing

شیمپو

The shampoo is used to clean your hair.

bulle

بلبلا

The bubbles are very fun to play in.

brosse

برش

She is brushing her hair with the brush.

papier toilette

ٹوائلٹ پیپر

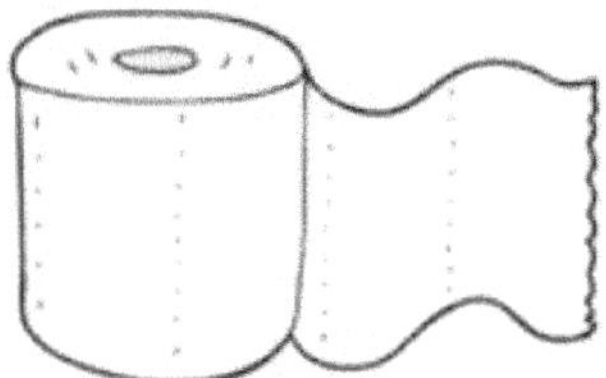

The toilet paper is used to dry your hands.

serviette

تولیہ

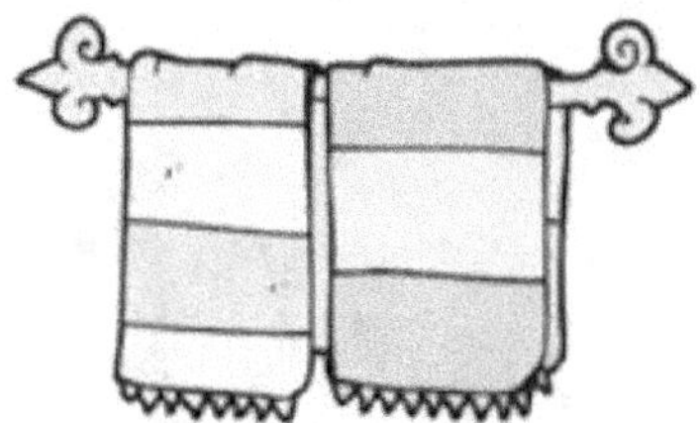

We have two towels on the rack.

corde à linge

کپڑے کی لائن

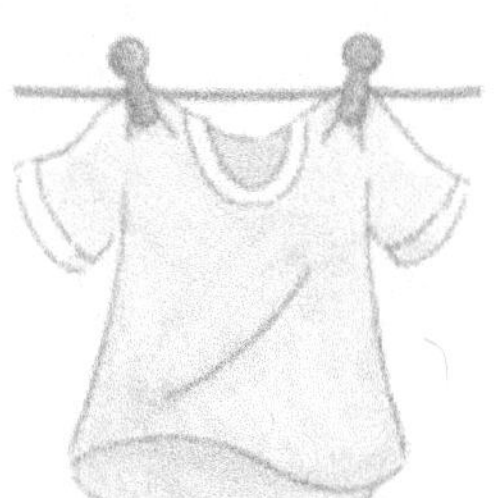

My shirt is hanging on the clothesline.

douche

شاور

The shower is spraying water.

baignoire

باتھ ٹب

The bathtub is comfortable.

lessive

لانڈری ڈٹرجنٹ

The laundry detergent is used with the washing machine.

seau

بالٹی

Can you help me fill up the bucket?

vadrouilles

موپس

The mop is used for mopping the floor.

savon liquide

مائع صابن

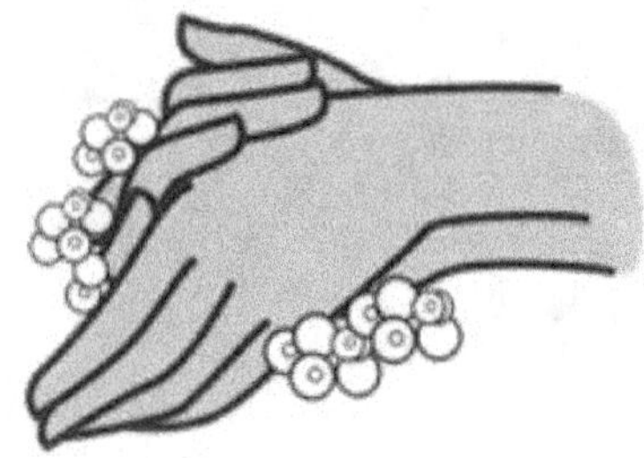

I use soapy water to wash my hands.

lessive en poudre

کپڑے دھونے کا صابن

I will scoop up the washing powder.

sac poubelle

کوڑے کا تھیلا

The trash bag is full of trash.

poubelle

کچرے دان

You have only to put recylcle trash in the trash can.

les puits

ڈوبتا ہے

You should wash your hands in the sink.

cuvette des toilettes

ٹوائلٹ کٹورا

She let her bunny use the toilet.

machine à laver

واشنگ مشین

The washing machine wash your clothes.

panier à linge

لانڈری کی ٹوکری

She is putting all the clothes into the laundry basket.

le rasoir

استرا

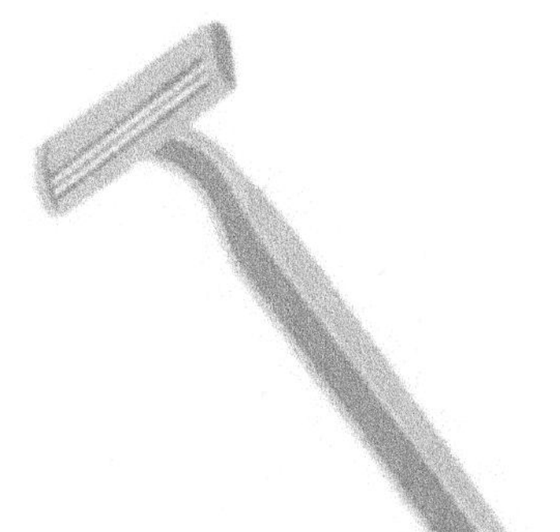

He uses the razor to shave his beard.

rasoir électrique

بجلی کا استرا

The electric razor works faster than the normal one.

crème à raser

مونڈنے کریم

The shaving cream is fluffy.

bain de bouche

ماؤتھ واش

The mouthwash smells very lovely.

coton-tige

روئی کی کلی

Q-tip can be used for many things.

brosse à cheveux

بالوں کا برش

She brushes her hair with her hairbrush.

peigne

کنگھی

Her dad will comb her hair for her.

nettoyant

صاف کرنے والا

Put the cap back on the cleanser bottle.

échelle

اسکیل

You can measure things on the scale.

papier de soie

ٹِشُو پیپر

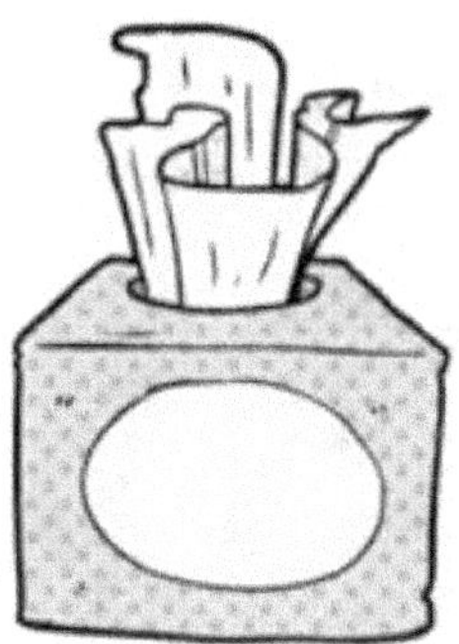

The tissue is on the counter.

jouets de bain

نہانے کے کھلونے

The little duck is a bath toy.

robinet

ٹونٹی

The faucet is broken.

miroir

آئینہ

He is looking in the mirror.

tapis de bain

غسل خانہ

The bath mat is purple and yellow.